Ladies of Grace

Promises for the Proverbs Woman

Iona —

Thanks for your support and friendship.

Linda Felker

Copyright © 2009 Dr. Linda F. Felker

ISBN 978-1-60145-799-8

All rights reserved. No part of this publication may be reproduced, stored in a retrieval system, or transmitted in any form or by any means, electronic, mechanical, recording or otherwise, without the prior written permission of the author.

Printed in the United States of America.

BookLocker.com, Inc.
2009

All Scripture References are from the King James Version (KJV) and the New International Version (NIV) of the Holy Bible.

Dedication

Many thanks to all the gracious ladies who contributed their promise verses and life stories to this book. It is our collective desire to use our experiences to encourage others.

Special thanks to my husband, Dave. Through many long months of preparation, study, writing, and editing, he has been there to help and support me in everything I needed.

And, to my mother, Mary Ruth Fox Day. You always set an example of continued faith. If ever there was a person who resembled the Proverbs Virtuous Woman, it is you.

Ladies of Grace
Promises for the Proverbs Woman
Table of Contents

Introduction	**1**
Promises for the Heart	**5**
Comfort	7
Faith	10
Forgiveness	13
Grace	16
Patience	18
Peace	22
Prayer	25
Rejoice	29
Promises for Life	**31**
Always With Us	33
Faithfulness	36
Help	39
His Presence	42
In Times of Trouble	47
Overcoming the World	51
Protection	53
Purpose	55
Strength	59
Trust	61
Promises for Family	**65**
Beautiful	67
Children	70

Parenting	72
Marriage	77
Sisterhood	79
The Greatest Promise of All	**83**
Salvation	85
Heaven	88
How to Find God's Promises	**90**
About The Author	**93**

Proverbs 31:10-31

"Who can find a virtuous woman? For her price is far above rubies.

The heart of her husband doth safely trust in her, so that he shall have no need of spoil.

She will do him good and not evil all the days of her life.

She seeketh wool and flax, and worketh willingly with her hands.

She is like the merchants ship; she bringeth her food from afar.

She riseth also while it is yet night, and giveth meat to her household, and a portion to her maidens.

She considereth a field, and buyeth it: with the fruit of her hands she planteth a vineyard.

She girdeth her loins with strength, and strengtheneth her arms.

She perceiveth that her merchandise is good; her candle goeth not out by night.

She layeth her hands to the spindle, and her hands hold the distaff.

She stretcheth out her hand to the poor; yea, she reacheth forth her hands to the needy.

She is not afraid of the snow for her household; for all her household are clothed with scarlet. She maketh herself coverings of tapestry; her clothing is silk and purple.

Her husband is known in the gates where he sitteth among the elders of the land.

She maketh fine linen, and selleth it, and delivereth it girdles unto the merchants.

Strength and honour are her clothing; and she shall rejoice in times to come.

She openeth her mouth with wisdom; and her tongue is the law of kindness.

She looketh well to the ways of her household; and eateth not the bread of idleness.

Her children arise up and call her blessed; her husband also, and he praiseth her.

Many daughters have done virtuously, but thou excelleth them all.

Favour is deceitful, and beauty is vain; but a woman that feareth the Lord, she shall be praised.

Give her the fruit of her hands; and let her own works praise her in the gates."

Introduction

When I began writing this book, I approached a friend at church and asked her if she would like to contribute her promise verse, and explained that I was using Proverbs 31 as the jumping off point for a book on women.

Her response? She said, *"Don't you just hate her? Who can be like that? And what's the deal with her husband, lying around in the gates all day while she's out in the fields toiling and working to feed the family!"*

Of course, she was joking, and we had a hearty laugh, and a good time talking about the example of the virtuous woman.

But, that conversation did make me wonder; are there women who do not understand the message God is trying to send us about our responsibilities as women?

I know that God would never give us an example of such a beautiful, accomplished, and loved virtuous woman as a tease and a torment, if we could never be that kind of person.

So, I began to study the scriptures. What is it about the woman described in Proverbs 31 that is different? What makes her special?

What are her characteristics and attributes? How can I have those same attributes working in my life? And, not only how, but where and what are the instructions?

The answers are contained in the verses themselves. I read each verse, and listed the attributes. Then, I searched the Bible to find what God said about those attributes.

Here is the amazing discovery. I found not only instructions; I found PROMISES! *"If I do this…, God will …!"*

Promises from God! Not only does He give us the expectations, He tells us how to do it, and then gives us a reward if we TRY! We are human, and we make mistakes.

However, we get credit for trying! I am not aware of any college or university in the world that gives you credit and rewards just for trying! Where's the mercy and grace there!

This book, "*Promises for the Proverbs Woman,*" steps through the attitudes and attributes of a virtuous woman. It looks at her characteristics and the promises associated with each one.

The highlights of this book are the personal testimonies and examples of women who have claimed these promises in their lives.

As I reached out to women, it was not because I necessarily knew of a critical time in their lives when they experienced a tragedy or triumph. The Holy Spirit hand-selected each person, and guided me to ask them the question, "*What is your promise verse? Would you be willing to share it with me, and also tell me about a time when God was faithful to you as you claimed that verse?*"

Every person I asked immediately said, "*Yes.*" There was no hesitation, and they provided me with their stories in very short order.

I believe God had already prepared their hearts, and although they did not know the purpose, they were waiting for an opportunity to share.

This kind of sisterhood, this depth of closeness between sisters in Christ is the catalyst for healing, change, and acceptance.

There are hurting people who need something to cling to just to make it through the day. Christian women are strong! They have fortitude. They have experienced Life! We can help each other, and lift each other up.

Therefore, to take the personal statements from these Godly women, and look at the characteristics of a virtuous woman, and then find the promises from God associated with the whole, was an exhilarating experience.

We can look at the life of the Proverbs woman and see specific focus areas for study. This book is divided into chapters that speak to those divisions.

Promises for the Heart is about a woman's heart and spirit. This is the place where all the action takes place, and where faith is found. This section of the book contains stories about comfort, forgiveness, joy, peace, and prayer along with other stories that will touch and encourage women.

Promises for Life gives directions for being a Christian in today's world. There are stories about overcoming, being faithful, and going through times of testing and trial.

Promises for the Family talks about children, husbands, parenting, and sisterhood. The virtuous woman was excellent at raising and providing for her children, being an exciting and helpful wife, while at the same time, taking care of the community and church.

T*he Greatest Promise of All* is the foundation of our lives through salvation by belief in our Lord Jesus Christ. It is a blessing to read about heaven, the reunion with loved ones, and best of all, our reunion with God.

God provided a way for all of us to be this woman through His word. His grace is evident as He shows us how to accomplish His will. Hebrews 10:23 *"Let us hold unswervingly to the hope we possess, for He who promised is faithful."* (KJV)

That's it! God will deliver on His promises to us if we are faithful.

What a great and mighty God we serve! How blessed to be under His arm of protection. My prayer is that we will all endeavor to be everything He wants us to be, and serve Him with gladness of spirit and thankful hearts.

The success of the Proverbs woman is her relationship to God.

Promises for the Heart

Comfort

Psalms 3:3 *"But Thou, O Lord, are a shield for me; my glory and the lifter up of my head."* (KJV)

God's comfort is an amazing thing, and hard to comprehend unless you have experienced a tragedy in your life like Wilma Sammons. She graciously agreed to share her promise verse and the reason why this verse means so much to her.

Wilma and her husband, Gary, are missionaries with Baptist Mid-Missions. This is her story.

"The verse, Romans 8:28, is the most vivid and special promise in God's Word for me. *"And we know that all things work together for good to them who love God, to them who are the called according to His purpose."* (KJV)

The power in this verse came to be the rock I held to when my 2 1/2 year old son, Paul Andrew Sammons, died. He was a beautiful little boy, healthy and strong.

It happened on a Sunday afternoon. Gary was the interim Pastor at a small church in rural Iowa. We had lunch with friends who lived on a small farm. Our son, Paul, had been enjoying seeing the animals and other things that would attract an inquisitive little boy.

The teenagers who had been playing with Paul, needed to attend to their chores, and no one brought Paul into the house to be with us. He fell into a small pool outside the back door. It did not look like a pool of water. It was covered with green algae, and we know that he thought he was stepping on grass, not water.

In a split second, he was ushered into the presence of the Lord.

When tragedy like this happens, our bodies go into shock. There is no time to search the scriptures to find help and encouragement.

At a time like this, the promises that have been hidden in our mind and heart come flooding to our souls, along with the sustaining grace that we need to face the situation.

We quote Romans 8:28 when wonderful things happen; when a car misses hitting us, when we do not lose our job yet a co-worker does, when a family member recovers from a terrible illness.

However, the scripture tell us that ALL things work together in His plan. Romans 8:28 MUST apply when the situation is full of grief and sorrow.

As I faced the death of my beautiful son, it was the assurance of Romans 8:28 that gave me the strength to go on.

ALL things will ULTIMATELY work together in the plan that God has for our lives.

Knowing that God's plan is ultimately perfect does not mean that painful things will not happen to us as Christians. The sorrow we experience still hurts, but there is comfort in knowing that an all-wise God is in total control.

The following quote by a Godly Christian leader of a large group of Baptist churches in America, Dr. Robert Ketchum, mirrors the truths of God's Word. This was written after the death of his wife and child:

"God is too good to be unkind and too wise to make a mistake."

Wilma's story is an incredible picture of God's grace. No doubt, the continual longing in her heart for her son will never truly end until she gets to Heaven. But, God's peace is upon her, and He has used her tremendously in His service.

Imagine the joyous day when she will be reunited with her precious son! Imagine God's joy when He was reunited with His precious son, Jesus Christ, after His death and resurrection.

God knows all about a broken heart. He knows what it feels like to lose a child – He understands.

All things – nothing excluded – everything – work together – not alone – for GOOD. Whose good? Our good and His good.

Psalms 147:3 *"Blessed are they that mourn; for they shall be comforted."* (KJV)

Psalms 34:18 *"The Lord is nigh unto them that are of a broken heart; and saves those who are crushed in spirit."* (KJV)

Faith

Matthew 17:20 "...*If ye have faith as a grain of mustard seed...nothing shall be impossible unto you.*" (NIV) I never saw a mustard seed, and did not know how small it was until one day while on vacation. We went shopping at an outlet mall. Outside the main stores were kiosk shops, each one selling different merchandise.

"*Hey Lady, do you wanna buy a necklace?*" A young man, about 16 or 17 years old, was standing beside a nearby kiosk, and holding several chains in his hand. It was his job to sell these trinkets, and he was asking everybody that walked by.

Not really wanting to buy a necklace, but feeling obligated to respond to his question, I stepped over to him and said, "*What kind of necklace is it?*"

"*Well, it's kinda like a silver chain with a pendant hanging on it,*" he replied.

"*What kind of pendant?*" I asked. Inwardly, I thought this young man was not a very good salesperson and did not seem to know his merchandise.

"*It's a mustard seed. I don't know much about them, but people like to buy them because of prayer.*"

I asked to hold the necklace, and looked at the tiny seed floating inside a round clear-glass pendant. The seed was so small! I wanted him to explain his comment about prayer.

So, I asked, "*What do you mean people buy them because of prayer?*"

Then he said, "*Well, I think that's why. I learned this Bible verse when I was a kid about having faith like a mustard seed. So, I guess that is why people buy them. They think God will answer their prayer if they have one.*"

His logic was somewhat understandable, however misinterpreted. I took a few moments to remind him of the exact words of the verse, Matthew 17:20, and explained that the verse was talking about having faith in God. It was not about wearing a mustard seed around our necks. And, I thanked him for his testimony.

He nodded as if he understood, then moved on to the next customer. As I walked away, I heard him tell the next person that, "*people like to buy the necklace with the mustard seed because it means they have faith."*

Michelle Sink is a woman whose life is built on faith. She often speaks of her desire to worship God in everything she does, and hopes to influence other women to activate their faith.

This is her Promise Verse on faith, and her explanation of why this verse is important in her life.

Philippians 1:6 *"Being confident of this very thing, that he which hath begun a good work in you will perform it until the day of Jesus Christ."* (KJV)

"Years ago, I heard someone speak on this subject. I was at a place in my life where I was searching and not sure which direction to go. This verse spoke to my heart and assured me.

Christ started a work in me, when I became a Christian at the age of seven. This verse gave me the assurance that He ultimately had a plan for my life. He would finish that plan that He began when I gave my life to Him.

When there are times in my life that I just do not understand, and I struggle with whether I am on the right path, I rest in this promise. He will finish what He started. I may not know how, but I know He is in control.

Over time, with my children growing up and seeing them make choices that I may not approve of, this verse has comforted me. I know for a fact that He started a plan in their lives.

There are times I do not understand their choices or their reasons. But, I **know** He will finish what He started in them. I have peace in that."

Hebrews 11:1 *"Faith is the substance of things hoped for, the evidence of things not seen."* (KJV)

As in Michelle's life, it is faith that allows us to follow God, even though we may not understand where He is taking us, and especially when life gets hard.

Faith is the opposite of fear, which can paralyze us and keep us from doing what God wants us to do. But, with God, all things are possible. As women of God, let us uphold other women and keep the faith flowing between us.

Unbelief causes heartache and pain. When you are facing something that seems impossible for you to overcome, remember that God is on your side. With Him, all things are possible. Stand steadfast in the faith, be strong, and watch what God will do in your life.

Jeremiah 32:27 *"Is there anything too hard to God?"* (KJV)

Forgiveness

Ephesians 4:31-32 *"Let all bitterness and wrath and anger and clamour and evil speaking be put away from you with all malice. And be ye kind one to another, tenderhearted, forgiving one another, even as God for Christ's sake hath forgiven you." (NIV)*

I love this promise, for without it, I would be eternally lost without God. It is only through Jesus Christ that we can find forgiveness and peace for our hearts.

My children heard me quote Ephesians 4:31 to them many times everyday. With each childhood squabble, with every disagreement, every harsh word, or hurt feelings, I quoted, *"...and be ye kind one to another..."*

Recently, I heard my daughter Marci telling a friend about it, and she said, *"My Mom ALWAYS used that verse – no matter what – even if it did not fit the situation!"*

I am so glad that she remembers. That is the whole point. I want my children to KNOW that God expects them to forgive each other and not hold grudges or bitterness in their hearts. To do so could ruin their lives!

1 John 1:9 *"If we confess our sins, he is faithful and just to forgive us our sins, and to cleanse us from all unrighteousness." (KJV)*

If God forgives us, and the price He paid for our sins was His only son Jesus Christ, who are we to refuse to forgive someone else?

People are human, and at times, they will disappoint and hurt us. Whether or not it is intentional, it still causes us pain.

However, God tells us to forgive them if we want to be forgiven.

Matthew 6:14-15 says, *"For if you forgive men of their trespasses, your heavenly father will also forgive you. But if you forgive men not their trespasses, neither will your Father forgive your trespasses."* (NIV)

This is HUGE! This should be enough to cause anyone to forgive anybody for anything at anytime! It is so easy to ask God to forgive us. But, we often find it hard to forgive other people.

This message was so important that Jesus repeated it again in Matthew 6: 14-15. In that scripture, He said, *"For if you forgive men when they sin against you, our Heavenly Father will also forgive you. But if you do not forgive men their sins, your Father will not forgive your sins."* (NIV)

This includes our enemies. However, it is much harder to forgive and **forget**. Only God can truly forget.

Isaiah 43:25 *"I, even I, am He that blotteth out thy transgressions for mine own sake, and will not remember thy sins."* (KJV)

We can try not to dwell on the past, or keep bringing things up again. When we harbor the past, it causes bitterness and grief in our hearts and minds. We cannot change the past, but we can learn from it.

God said in Isaiah 43:18 *"Forget the former things; do not dwell on the past."* (NIV)

Who is the hardest person for you to forgive? Is it your husband, child, friends, parents? No! It is yourself. We ask for God's forgiveness, and then literally throw it back at Him when we do not accept it. Instead, we continue to carry the guilt with us like a shield, and measure everything in our lives by that one incident.

It is like telling God that His forgiveness was not good enough to cover our sin; the sacrifice of His son was not enough.

We allow the enemy, Satan, to torment us with thoughts of our past sin. We cling to it, and ask God repeatedly to forgive us. It is time to stop!

Let go of the baggage you are carrying in your life. God casts our sins as far as the East is from the West! Psalms 103:11-13 *"For as high as the heavens are above the earth, so great is his love for those who fear him; as far as the east is from the west, so far has he removed our transgressions from us. As a father has compassion on his children, so the Lord has compassion on those who fear him."* (KJV)

He forgets our sins! Our Lord delights in showing us mercy. We must also stop judging and condemning ourselves, and others.

See yourself as God see you - fully loved and truly forgiven.

Grace

2 Corinthians 9:8 *"And God is able to make all grace abound to you, so that in all things at all times, having all that you need, you will abound in every good work."* (KJV)

Look carefully at this verse. In **all things**, at **all times**, God gives us grace. Not just a little bit of grace. Abounding grace; flourishing and thriving. True grace is powerful, and a precious gift from God that blesses His children, while at the same time, glorifies Him..

It is only through God's grace that we have salvation through Jesus Christ. I am so thankful that God does not deal with me like I truly deserve, but through eyes of mercy and abounding grace.

When I fail miserably, God's amazing grace restores me. When I need comfort and a touch from God to soothe my hurting heart, He is always there. So it is with all His children. He abundantly and freely gives grace in our lives.

Lois Horton is incredibly talented, and uses her musical ability to reach adults and children for Christ. She is a warm and loving person, who inspires others with her sincerity and desire to serve the Lord.

This is her story and promise verse, which reflects the continuing work of grace in her life.

"My journey as a daughter of Jehovah God has been filled with all kinds of situations and circumstances that have tested and ultimately grown my faith in my heavenly Father.

God's grace helped me to triumph victoriously over thoughts of, not just taking my own life, but also taking the life of another. My family has faced financial challenges, catastrophic illness, near fatal accidents, and the list goes on.

When life got hard, I would always cling to God's promises in Proverbs 3:5&6 and Romans 8:28, and spend time reflecting on the faithfulness of God to our family in the past. This was always sufficient to get me through to the calmer side of any situation.

However, eight years ago I found myself facing a personal situation that left me confused and frightened. I was unable to rest in the promises in which I had always found comfort. When I prayed, I just could not hear God.

At 5:30 a.m. on the morning of the day that I was to come face-to-face with some of my worst fears, I cried out to God in the darkness of my room, *"Father, I am so afraid. I can't hear your voice of comfort at all, and I need You. Please help me. Please help me now!"*

At that very moment, my phone rang. I answered it. It was a very dear friend of mine, and she said, *"Lois, I have a verse that God wants you to read this morning. Get your Bible and read Isaiah 41:13. That's your verse. God loves you. I love you and I will be praying for you."*

We hung up, and I reached for my Bible, turned to Isaiah 41:13 and read it: *"For I am the Lord, your God, who takes hold of your right hand and says to you, 'Do not fear; I will help you.'"* (NIV)

Instantly, a peace washed over my very soul. My Heavenly Father was going to hold my hand and help me! I quickly memorized that verse and spoke it many times over the course of the events to follow.

God's promise in Isaiah 41:13 has brought me peace and comfort many times since that day. Once again, my God had not just comforted me for one time, but gave me an assurance of His grace and love that would last to eternity.

Praise God for His unfailing love and His forever promises!"

Patience

Psalms 27:14 *"Wait on the LORD: be of good courage, and he shall strengthen thine heart: Wait, I say, on the LORD."* (KJV)
A strong heart! God does not want us to live in despair, disappointment, or fear, but to lean on Him.

Moreover, He wants us to understand that our timetable may not be the same as His. He wants us to WAIT on Him. That's a hard one for us to do because we want it *now*. This is especially true when we have a deep need or desire, or we are in pain or afraid. We do not want to wait.

As we wait on the answer from the Lord, we should show strength and courage in our lives, and remember that we are setting an example for others. Our demeanor and behavior will either be a good witness for the Lord, or damage our credibility as a Christian.

A strong heart is one that does not when faced with sorrow, fear, or pain. We can claim His promise that He will never leave us or forsake us. We may go through the fire, but He is there with us.

Life is 10% what happens to us, but 90% how we take it. He will give us courage to sustain us through tremendous times of longing and loss.

This is especially true in the life of Ruth McPhaul. This is her story.

"My husband Mike and I were married in 1991, and I knew that I wanted to have a family someday. I loved children and always wanted to be a "mommy' when I grew up.

After being married five years, I began praying to have a baby. I claimed the verse, Psalms 37:4, which says, *"Delight thyself also in the Lord; and He shall give thee the desires of thine heart."* (KJV) I memorized this verse and asked the Lord everyday to give me the desire of my heart...a baby.

After trying to conceive on our own for some time, we tried using medications and other procedures to help start our family. That did not work, and the doctor finally told us that our chances of having a baby were less than 1/2%. This was heartbreaking news. I kept thinking about the verse that promised me He would give me the desire of my heart.

Mike and I made a decision to stop the treatments, and just give this to the Lord. I claimed the verse Psalms 27:14B, *"Wait, I say, on the Lord."* (KJV)

Three years later, I found out I was pregnant. Without any help, except the Lord's help! Finally, the Lord was giving me the desire of my heart.

Our son, Allen Battle McPhaul, was born on June 23, 2004 (3 months early) with Diaghragmatic Hernia. He only lived 12 hours. I could not understand why the Lord gave me the desire of my heart and then took it away so quickly.

The night that Allen passed away was so difficult. We were called to the NICU around 10:30 p.m. because the Doctor said that Allen would not live much longer. We called Pastor Sears and he came quickly.

Mike and I talked to a Doctor from Baptist Hospital about the possibility of donating Allen's organs. We felt that if he was not going to live, maybe he could help other babies. The Doctor told us that Allen was just too premature for the donation, but he appreciated our thoughts.

The nurses came to us around 11:30 p.m. and told us that they needed to disconnect Allen's tubes so we could hold him one last time. I could not stay there and watch that being done to my son; so, Pastor Sears wheeled me to my room. Mike was allowed to carry Allen from the NICU to our room.

He held him for several minutes and then handed Allen to me. I held him so close and tight, knowing I would never see him grow up and be part of our family here on earth.

While I was holding him, the Doctor came over to check his heartbeat. She heard it getting slower and slower until he passed away at 12:12 a.m.

I did not cry a lot at first, because I was in such shock. I was thankful that I got to hold him while he was still alive. My parents were called and they arrived after Allen had passed away. It was such a sad time to see my "desire" go, but deep down, I knew that I would see him again and spend an eternity with him.

That night, I took a sleeping pill so that I could get some rest. As morning came, the Doctor decided to let me go home a day early so that I would not have to hear all the babies crying in the rooms around me. He felt that I would be able to get more rest at home.

When I got in the car to leave, I felt such emptiness. When you have a baby, and go home from the hospital, you are supposed to be happy and have a baby in the back seat of the car. It was such a deep sadness to go home empty-handed.

I went back to the Bible and found the verse Romans 8:28 *"And we know that all things work together for good to them that love God, to them who are the called according to his purpose."* (KJV)

I also found comfort in the verse Hosea 14:9 *"...for the ways of the Lord are right."* (KJV)

We had to claim that the Lord was in control and believe that He made no mistakes. We found out later that three people who had asked, *"What happen to Allen; why did he die so young?"* had accepted Christ. We realized that the short time our son Allen had been here, he had fulfilled what the Lord had planned for him.

Four years later, we found out that we were expecting another baby. Another miracle from the Lord.

Audrey Elizabeth, born on August 2, 2008, is perfectly healthy. She is the delight of my heart each and every day. I thank the Lord for giving us this child, and on August 3, we celebrated our 17th wedding anniversary.

"Wait, I say, on the Lord."

Peace

Philippians 4:6-7 *"Be careful for nothing, but in everything by prayer and supplication with thanksgiving let your requests be made known unto God. And the peace of God, which passeth all understanding, shall keep your hearts and minds through Christ Jesus."* (KJV)

God does not expect us to go through life with a tense inner anguish, and worrying about things over which we have no control. Nor does He want us to doubt His power and majesty.

He told us in His word to lean on Him, and He would give us peace as we obey His word and claim His promises. Doris West is a great example of this principle.

She stayed faithful to the Lord, even though her husband was unsaved. By continuing to petition God in prayer for her husband, and raise her children for the Lord, God answered her prayer.

Today, Doris and Charles West are responsible for winning many others to the Lord through their obedient lives and faithful testimony.

This is Doris' story.

"My Mother made an impression on my life in many ways as I was growing up. I was saved and baptized in my early teenage years. However, after I graduated from high school, I drifted away from church and out of fellowship with God.

I married Charles West and we had two children: DeAnne, and Chuck. They attended Salem Baptist Day School. DeAnne was saved at the age of nine and Chuck at the age of seven.

DeAnne, Chuck, and I visited several churches, and I was determined to keep them in church where they could learn and grow, just as my Mother did for me. I started praying for my husband Charles to be saved.

One week, we visited Grace Baptist Temple. The people were friendly, and we heard the gospel preached. I knew I was where God had led us.

Romans 8:38-39 *"For I am persuaded that neither death, nor life, nor angels, nor principalities, nor powers, nor things present, nor things to come, nor height, nor depth, nor any other creature, shall be able to separate us from the love of God, which is in Christ Jesus our Lord."* (KJV)

I clung to that verse, and continued to take my children to church, while praying that God would get hold of my husband's heart. Although I was regularly attending church at Grace, I did not want to join the church until our entire family was saved and joined together.

One night, Pastor Sears came to our home, shared the gospel through scripture, and led Charles to the Lord. He was saved! We went to church as a family, and were all baptized together. I rededicated my life to the Lord, and have been so thankful for His encouragement and fulfillment of His promises in my life.

Without Him, our family would not be complete in the Lord."

Doris and her family experienced the Peace that only God can give. Many years have passed since the West family joined Grace Baptist Temple, and they have been years of faithful service to our Lord.

John 14:27 *"Peace I leave with you, my peace I give unto you; not as the world giveth, give I unto you. Let not your heart be troubled, neither let it be afraid."* (KJV)

What a precious promise! No matter what is going on in our lives or in the world around us, God is in control. Naturally, that includes our families; but it also includes those things that form our existence.

God is in charge of world leaders, world economy, bailouts, and every other situation known to man. Nothing takes God by surprise. He is in control.

There is no reason for us to worry about what is going on around us, or what is coming our way tomorrow.

The promise verse says, *"Peace I give unto you…and don't be troubled or afraid."*

Prayer

Matthew 21:22 *"And all things, whatsoever ye shall ask in prayer, believing, ye shall receive."* (NIV)

Wednesdays nights are hectic at our house. The grandchildren, Zachary and Jackson, usually arrive around 4:30, and I cook whatever they would like to eat for the evening meal.

Jackson, who is five years old, loves beef stew and rice, but not in that order. He always reminds me to put the rice on the plate first, and then pile the beef stew on top. Zachary, eight years old, likes vegetables, and usually asks for okra, green beans, corn, and chicken.

It is such a pleasure to have them with me, and I take advantage of every moment. I ask about their day at school, what is going on with the Little League team, and whatever else they want to talk about.

Zachary usually has homework, and I enjoy working with him and listening to him read. Then, I help Jackson memorize his Bible verses for Awana's Sparks Club at our church, which begins at 6:45 p.m.

It is a flurry of activity for two hours, and I wish I had longer! Nonetheless, we usually manage to get it all done, and get to church on time.

As we drive to church, we play car games, such as *I Spy*, and *Rhyming*. I want to take advantage of every minute I have with these little boys. Sometimes, as we drive to church, I use the time to recite the Bible verse once more with Jackson.

One Wednesday evening, the verse was about prayer, and I repeated the verse several times.

"That doesn't work", declared Jackson.

"What doesn't work?" I asked.

"Prayer. It doesn't work." he stated in a very matter-of-fact way.

"Jackson, why would you say that prayer does not work." I said.

"I know it doesn't; I just know," he replied.

"Tell me why you feel that way. What did you pray about that God did not answer?"

Jackson immediately said, *"Well, I prayed to be Spiderman, but I'm still here!"*

He said this with a flair of drama, waving his arms toward the sky as if begging God to do something about this special request!

Children have such a literal perception of everything in their realm of reality. Jackson had been taught that God answers prayer; therefore, he believed that whatever he asked for, he would get.

It was hard not to laugh, and he was so serious! Remaining composed was critical! His little face turned toward mine with a quizzical look, I just wanted to stop the car and wrap him in a big hug and hold him forever.

Later that evening at church, I told my friend, Lucretia Chitty, what Jackson had said. Lucretia is a kindergarten teacher at a local Christian School.

She said, *"Well, just tell him that God does answer our prayers, but not always in the way we want Him to. Sometimes he says yes; sometimes He says no; and sometimes He tells us to wait a while."*

What have you prayed about lately? Do you feel that God answered your prayer? The verse, Matthew 21:22, does not mean that we will receive everything we ask for. But, it does mean that, if it is God's will, it will happen.

After all, we might ask for something that would hurt us. We do not know what is waiting in the future, but God knows. He is looking at all His children, and answers our prayers based on His will and perfect timing.

One day, we may be thankful that God said "*no*" to a request. We can always be assured that, when we pray, He will hear.

During the summer, while the Awana Club is on break, our church has Vacation Bible School on Wednesday nights. Zachary and Jackson enjoy attending VBS, hearing the Bible stories, making crafts, and having a snack.

One evening, I took the boys to their VBS room, and turned to walk down the hall to choir practice. Zachary came running out of his classroom behind me, and sat down on the bench just beyond the Welcome Center.

I heard him behind me, and immediately joined him on the bench, asking if he was all right. My first thought was that he was sick.

"*Zachary, what's wrong? Don't you feel well? Why did you leave your classroom*?" I bombarded the child with questions without waiting for a reply.

My left arm slipped around his shoulders, and I pulled him close to me, while my right hand felt his forehead to determine if he had a fever.

"*I can't go in there. I want to go home.*" That was all he said. He did not answer any of my questions.

"*But, Zachary,*" I said, "*God wants you to be in VBS with your friends so that you can...*"

That was as far as I got. Zachary looked at me almost angrily, and shouted, "*Don't say that to me. I'm not going to Heaven like you.*"

Shocked, my grip tightened on those little shoulders, and I said, "*Zachary, do you want to go to Heaven? You can be saved right now, right this minute, if you just talk to God.*"

He was holding on tight to his little children's Bible, the one with the picture of Jesus on the cover, surrounded by children.

He held the Bible up to me, and said, "*Show me in here. Show me where it says that.*"

I prayed quietly in my spirit for God to give me the words

to lead this most precious child to Him.

Gripping the little Bible, I found Romans 3:23, *"For all have sinned and come short of the glory of God."* (KJV)

Then, I read John 3:16. *"For God so loved the world that He gave His only begotten Son; that whosoever believeth in Him should not perish, but have everlasting life."* (KJV)

I explained God's love, and the plan of salvation in words I thought he child would understand.

"Zachary, do you want to ask Jesus to come into your heart right now?"

"Yes!" he replied with certainty. God had already prepared His heart for this moment. I prayed, and Zachary prayed.

It did not matter that we were sitting on a metal bench in Welcome Center of the church. It did not matter how many people walked by, or what was going on all around us.

At that moment, Zachary received Jesus as His Savior.

Oh, what a great blessing God gave me to allow me to lead Zachary to Him.

The next day, Zachary and Jackson were at my house along with their father, my son Todd. My daughter, Marci was there, as well as our youngest son, Brent.

As we gathered around the dining room table, I asked Zachary if he would like to say the blessing before we ate.

Zachary said, *"Nana, with all that praying I did yesterday, it's somebody else's turn!"*

Funny? Yes! We laughed and thought he was so cute. Yet, his words are astoundingly true.

It is someone else's turn to pray for salvation. The world is full of people who need the Lord. Search your heart; do you find Jesus there? Have you ever asked him to come into your life as Lord and Savior?

Today is your day; this is your hour.

Acts 16:31 *"Believe on the Lord Jesus Christ, and thou shalt be saved."* (KJV)

Rejoice

I've got the joy, joy, joy, joy down in my heart! Where? Down in my heart. Where? Down in my heart. I've got the joy, joy, joy, joy down in my heart. Where? Down in my heart to stay!"

This happy child's song talks about the everlasting joy in our lives that comes from knowing Christ.

Job 8:21 *"He will yet fill your mouth with laughter and your lips with shouts of joy."* (KJV)

Life is not something to be endured, but a gift to be truly appreciated. Intense, happy, successful, BIG life!

I do not want to miss a thing that God has planned for me, and I long for that deep, fulfilling kind of joy that only comes from being in God's will.

Have you lost your joy? Has your life become routine, with no sparkle or snap? How sad and dreary it would be to go through live without passion and purpose, without joy.

Women tend to take themselves much too seriously. Many of us do not know how to overcome stress, and are especially prone to suffer from depression. Perhaps we fill our lives by trying to be 'everything to everyone else', and neglect ourselves and the purpose God's established for us.

Lighten up! It is amazing the tools you receive from the Lord to reduce your stress when you choose to be happy and content.

Psalm 18:46 *"The Lord liveth; and blessed be my rock; and let the God of my salvation be exalted."* (NIV)

We are His delight, and He gave each of us unique gifts and talents with which to serve Him. There is no reason to allow negativity and sadness of spirit to invade your heart and mind.

Psalms 16:11 *"You will make known to me the path of life; in Your presence is fullness of joy."* (NIV)

The Lord's joy is found in His presence, like a gift. Even though we may enjoy people and things in our lives, only God gives us everlasting joy.

The joy of the Lord is powerful. In John 15:11, it is described as complete, and in Psalms 43:4 it is filling. In Psalms 35:10, it is everlasting and overwhelming.

Do you know the natural gifts and talents the Lord gave you? What are you doing with them? Do you know what God is calling you to do?

It does not have to be what we consider huge sacrifices, or traveling around the world in His service. You can serve Him right where you are. But, until we open our hearts and spirits, and listen for His voice, we may never know the true joy that comes from being in His will.

Psalms 16:11 *"You will make known to me the path of life; In Your presence is fullness of joy . . ."* (NIV)

The joy of the Lord is a fruit of the Spirit, as stated in Galatians 5:22. It is intended to be shared. When we pour out our joy through our lives, we give joy to others.

Have you ever noticed how hard it is to be down when you are around someone who is full of joy?

Allow the Holy Spirit to live in you and always guard your joy. The enemy wants you to be overwhelmed and overtaken by your own or someone else's negative comments, thoughts, and actions.

Hold on tight to the joy of the Lord. It is your divine and most precious strength. It will keep your hearts alive, even when in the midst of despair.

Hebrews 12:1 *"Wherefore seeing we also are compassed about with so great a cloud of witnesses, let us lay aside every weight, and the sin which doth so easily beset us, and let us run with patience the race that is set before us."* (KJV)

Promises for Life

Always With Us

Matthew 28:20 *"...lo I am with you always, even unto the end of the world."* (KJV)

There may be times in our lives when we feel alone, and that we have more on us that we can bear. Health problems, family issues, and troubles in this world can crash about us without warning.

Always remember that God is faithful to His children. He will never leave us alone. We can find assurance in His word, and know that He loves and cares for us. Just as He fulfilled His promises to so many mighty men and women throughout the scriptures, He will do the same for us. Rebecca Nordlander is an inspiration to women everywhere, and a testimony of God's love. She experienced a terrifying illness, yet never failed to smile and express her praise for His sustaining presence in her life.

Rebecca's experience reminds us that God is the one true absolute in our lives if we have trusted Him as our Lord and Savior.

This is her story.

"When I was a child I used to think that a potter was probably a very poor person who had very little, and who made a living by making things from mud.

Later in life, I learned that the potter is one of the most respected merchants in town. Pottery is used in every home. Not only is the potter talented in shaping many different things, he is wise in selecting and using the various different clays.

Some types of clay make delicate items, while other clays are stronger for the sturdy and durable pieces. But, all must go through a time of shaping and being in the fiery oven before they can be used.

In 2006, as we were praying in my office at Piedmont Baptist College, I asked the Lord for revival in our church, and I half-seriously said, "*Start with me. There is not much to work with, but I'm willing to be used.*" Little did I know what was in store for me.

As always, in September I went for my yearly mammogram. One of the technicians seemed to be a little nervous. I remember thinking that I would probably be called back in for a re-do.

All women know what a re-do is. Sure enough, I received the call and went back into the office for a second time. The technician said that the film did not give her a clear picture and she needed to do it again. After the re-do, I had to wait again, and then the technician said the doctor needed a sonogram.

I grew impatient and I asked her why. She muttered something, but did not give me a clear answer. It did not take me long to wonder what was going on. I lay on the table, and she began the process. She focused on a certain spot and kept searching until a big black spot came up on the screen. I saw it and I thought, "*What's that?*"

She measured the spot and then moved to take a run at it from a different angle. Again, the spot appeared and again she measured it.

That is when the potter's wheel began to turn. I realized that they had found a lump in my breast, and my world began to spin. My mind swirled and I thought, "*Lord, is this cancer? Is this really happening to me? How can I even begin to tell my husband, my children, and my family what is happening?*"

Then my mind raced to my grandbaby boys. "*Oh Lord, my grandbaby boys? Lord, please. I want to live to see them grow up and serve you. Lord, please help me!*" The wheel seemed to be turning faster and faster and I felt like I was surely going to spin out of control.

At that very moment, I cried out to God. He heard me, and the potter's hands went around this old lump of clay, and said,

"Becky, I'm here. Be not afraid. As I promised, I will never leave you or forsake you. Do you remember asking me to use you? Well, I heard your prayer and wish to use you. I am here and I will be with you through it all. Don't be afraid."

I thought, *"But Lord, I am so scared. I've never faced anything like this before and I don't know if I can. I do not think I have what it takes to go through this. Please forgive my lack of faith and help me. Please hold my hand through this."*

He quietly said, *"I'll do better than that. I will hold you in the palm of my hand."* (Isaiah 41:13). Though the wheel kept spinning, I felt his hands surround me, holding me fast, and my heart began to be at peace.

I have no doubt that I received a precious touch of grace from the Lord. If I live to be 100 years old, I may never experience that moment again. What a blessing.

The months that followed were full of x-rays, scans, operations, chemotherapy treatments, and radiation. The prayers of people who continually lifted my name before the Father sustained me.

Times were hard, but I learned so much. I neither resent nor regret having gone through this trial.

Yes, the potter's wheel is still spinning, but I can truly say that the Lord has been with me through it all. He has been my comforter, my healer, and my tower of strength. To Him be all the glory."

Faithfulness

Years ago, I taught the three-to-five year-old Sunday School Class at our church. Every week, I used the flannel-graph board to tell a Bible story, and worked with the children to memorize their Bible verses.

I loved those children; I loved teaching that class. During those years, I had the honor of teaching my own children. There were so many precious little ones in that room every Sunday morning, and we had such fun together.

One week, a new little boy attended the class. He was special from the minute he walked through the door, all dressed up in a suit and tie, and carrying a HUGE Bible.

He was a natural fit with this class from the first minute. The other children accepted him into the group, and he immediately became part of them, as if they were siblings. And, all the little girls in the class just loved sitting next to Brian Spence.

Brian could recite his Bible verse with no help from me at all. After I met his mother, Phyllis, I knew why. It was apparent that she was a hands-on Mom who not only took care of Brian physically; she was preparing him spiritually for the day when God would touch his heart.

From the outside looking in, some people might have thought that Phyllis lived a charmed life. She had a lovely home, tremendous musical talent, loving husband; all the "things" that people find appealing.

Her life, however, was not perfect, although many people did not realize the trial and testing that she was experiencing. Her body was going through a dramatic and painful disease, but Phyllis was determined to continue serving the Lord fully.

Many times, her husband, Guy, would help her up to the platform to sing; then, he would help her back down. It was not an option for Phyllis to stop; she kept going, and God rewarded her faithfulness.

Phyllis and I have been friends for twenty-eight years now, and God has been faithful to us as we have raised our children, faced life's challenges, and experienced His joy.

This is her story.

Galatians 2:20 '*I am crucified with Christ: nevertheless I live; yet not I, but Christ liveth in me: and the life which I now live in the flesh I live by faith of the Son of God, who loved me, and gave Himself for me.*' (KJV)

"We were on a family vacation and chose to attend a local worship service on Sunday morning. That was where I first heard 'my verse' read by the pastor of this small church. I took that verse right then as my verse. Now, for some 30-plus years, my choice for my life's verse has been proven time and time again.

I want my life to be a constant refection of Christ living through me, not me living through Him.

One day, I reached to pick up a cast iron frying pan. The pain that ran through my thumb was unbearable. I first thought something had stung me.

Over time, that pain affected my entire body. I had difficulty sitting for any length of time. I had to have help in order to rise from a chair. My husband had to help me get in and out of bed. During the night, he helped me get into another position in order to relieve the pain.

At times, I could not eat because of the intense pain in my jaw-joints. My doctor gave me a handicap sticker and advised me to get a wheel chair. I took his sticker but not his advice about the wheel chair; I just could not bring myself to go there until I had to.

For several months, I was treated for Rheumatoid Arthritis. With time, the condition became much more violent. I quoted my verse many times throughout this long, painful ordeal, which ultimately lasted several years. I would live by the faith that my verse said was mine.

I was sent to a very prominent Rheumatologist in our city. He admitted me to the hospital and there they found that my condition was known as Poly-mio-citis, a very rare form of arthritis, affecting only four in a million people.

"Why me, Lord?"

If the Doctors had not discovered that I had this disease, it would have certainly taken my life. It affects every joint, all connective tissue, and every muscle in the body.

Since the heart is a muscle, it would ultimately have affected my heart. With massive Prednisone treatments, the disease is now in remission, and for that, I am truly thankful to God. Today I have absolutely no signs of Poly-mio-citis!

I lived my life knowing that my faith would see me through, no matter what the outcome, and it has."

Deuteronomy 7:9 *"The Lord your God is the Faithful God."* (KJV)

Help

Psalms 121:1-2 *"I will lift up mine eyes to the hills, from whence cometh my help. My help cometh from the Lord, which made heaven and earth."* (KJV)

Friday, March 29, 1996, began for Paula Stant much like any other day. She awoke with songs from the Easter Cantata ringing in her head. She was looking forward to the evening performance, yet dreading the costume of biblical robes and headgear.

Oh, that dreaded headgear! How did they ever keep those shawls on their heads and get anything done back in Biblical times.

Paula describes the subsequent events of that day with sincerity and honesty. This is her story.

"After working until noon, I took a half-day off to buy groceries before preparing supper for my family. I looked forward to my youngest son's visit from college.

Upon arriving home, my telephone was ringing. Rushing to answer it, I heard a pause, followed by my youngest brother's voice. *"Hi, Paula. How are you?"*

"Fine," I replied, *"how are things there?"*

"I have some not so good news. Mom and Dad were on their way home from Art's (my oldest brother) when their car was hit by a truck. <u>They are both gone</u>."

I only remember sliding down the wall and loudly exclaiming *"No!"*

Then I heard Daniel say, *"Are you all right?"*

Was I all right? It was unreal. *"Are you sure – have you seen them?"*

"No, I'm just telling you what the police told me. Their bodies have been positively identified by their driver's licenses

and they are being transported here at this time. You will have to come; we need you. There are many decisions to be made. I'm depending on you to take care of letting Becky know."

Then the responsibilities began. I pled with my heavenly Father to guide me. I started quoting scriptures in my spirit.

Hebrews 13:5 *"I will never leave you."* (KJV)

Romans 8:38-39 *"Death cannot separate you from the love of God."* (KJV)

Psalm 121:1 *"I will look unto the hills from which cometh my help."* (NIV)

Coming from a great Christian family, being a pastor's daughter, and the eldest child, brought with it a lot of responsibility. My father engraved in me my position as the eldest.

My sister Becky and I were scheduled to perform in the cantata at church in just a few hours. When we were asked what we were going to do about the cantata, we answered that we would be there! And, we were there, in full costume! We sang and performed in the cantata as planned before the accident. It is what our parents would have wanted us to do.

There is nothing as important as the Lord's Darling, the church. We had always been taught, and still believe, that our first responsibility is to the Lord's church.

I cannot neglect to tell you of the wonderful love shown us by our Pastor and Grace Baptist Temple. That evening, there was a tray of food delivered. The next morning, transportation was provided to take Becky, my daughter Angela, and me to Syracuse, NY.

We sang all of our parents' favorite songs on the way to New York, and recounted the many adventures afforded us in our lives all across this nation.

The next week was a blur. There were so many decisions to be made, brochures to be written, and songs to be sung. We took care of all the preachers who traveled to be there to speak at the funeral.

We enjoyed the revival meeting called a "funeral", and then had to leave my parents at the gravesite in a holding area because the ground was frozen. We took care of their meager belongings, and then returned home, where I had to really face life again.

Did I grieve for my parents? No, I grieved for me. They *"woke up and found Heaven home."* Their prayers were answered; they left this world together. I would miss them tremendously, but I never felt forsaken. I had my Heavenly Father to uphold me. The memories play constantly in my busy life, and mostly, they bring a smile and comfort even during the rough times.

I will always miss them. The older I get, the more I look forward to seeing them again in Heaven - my beautiful mother and my strong reliable father."

His Presence

Statistics tell us that one of the greatest fears that people have is the fear of being left alone. Ever since the beginning of time, when Adam and Eve sinned and were evicted from the Garden of Eden, the human race has had a fear of being alone and forever separated from God.

Jesus Christ came into the world to reconcile us to God. When we accept Him, we will never be alone again. We have God's promise of his love and care of us everyday of our lives.

Hebrews 13:5 *"Never will I leave you; never will I forsake you."* (NIV)

His Presence is always with us; however, the manner in which He chooses to reveal Himself to us is different for every person.

Phyllis Redding tells the story of God's presence in her life, and relates the exact moment when she "saw" Him. Her humor and wit will encourage your heart as you read her promise verse and her story.

John 15:16 *"Ye have not chosen me, but I have chosen you, and ordained you, that ye should go and bring forth fruit, and that your fruit should remain; that whatsoever ye ask of the Father in my name, He may give it to you."* (NIV)

"I did not know that I did not have it until I got it. When I got it, then I knew that I never had it before! But now, I know I do!

I gave my heart to Jesus when I was seventeen. Twenty years later, I made a new friend, Carole, at work. I was desperate to "save" her. We talked, and I gave her a Bible. I prayed for her, and thought surely I could teach her, and lead her to Christ.

Oh, how I wanted to drag her to a baptismal pool and hold her under until I saw bubbles! She would have none of it *"my way*". She was not familiar with the word *"saved"*, and said that was a Southern term.

In the meantime, my marriage was falling apart. He was a Christian; I was a Christian, and we had been going to church together for fourteen years. Yet, our marriage was ending, and I began to steadily drift away from God and church.

Twenty more years passed, and then I was 57 years old (forty years after I accepted Christ Jesus as my Savior.) God used Carole to draw me back to Him. During these years, Carole had grown in her relationship with the Lord.

She had been asking me, "*What's going on with you?*" I knew she meant spiritually, and I would tell her that nothing in particular was happening. She would not let it go, and was really beginning to get on my nerves!

Irritated, I sent her an email that "He" was not doing anything special in my life. I assured her that if anything happened, she would be the first to know! I even sent her the scripture Philippians 4:11, "*I am content in my present circumstances.*" (NIV)

However, what Carole _received_ was Philippians 4:10, which says, "*I rejoice in the Lord greatly that now at last you have renewed your concern for me.*" Wrong! I did NOT send that message! How did that happen?

Carole replied in an email that she "needed" me. She had always been a very independent woman; what did she mean that she needed me? I began to imagine all sorts of terrible things that might be wrong with her. Maybe she had some dreadful disease; maybe even terminal. Maybe there was a problem with her marriage.

I agreed to carve out a four-day weekend to spend with her. My friend needed me, and I had to be there for her.

Carole and I and drove to Surf City, a small beach area of North Carolina, where she had the tiniest little trailer that she had remodeled.

There was a strange, unusual quietness between us that went on for much too long. It was awkward. I kept waiting for her to tell me about her problem.

Finally, to fill the void, I began telling her about my neighbor who had asked me to pray for her regarding an upcoming operation. I confessed to Carole that I was holding a grudge against my friend, and I knew I could not pray for my neighbor without first asking forgiveness for myself, and forgiving my friend.

Then, it began. Carole, who did not know her way around the Bible as well as I did, who did not know Job from job, reached for her Bible and said, *"Let's see what the Bible says about forgiveness."*

The Holy Spirit took over. Carole became the teacher and I was the student. She went scripture to scripture about forgiveness, and she read aloud to me, as if I was a child.

This went on into the early evening. We stopped long enough to eat, then began again. And, I saw Jesus. There were no loud symbols, no trumpets, no bolts of lightening, no burning bush, no passing out. It wasn't a dream. It wasn't like a vision or like some scene cast upon the living room wall.

It was a ***knowing***, from somewhere deep inside me. His love just turned my heart to mush. I saw Jesus in my heart and mind. I ***knew*** how much He loved me! I am sure it was only a glimpse of His love, and at that, I was overwhelmed!

You see, I thought I knew what being a Christian was all about. Having been *"saved"* at seventeen, I knew it all, even if I never read my Bible or prayed except when I was in trouble.

I used God like a spare tire, only when I was flat out of excuses, or time; or needed an escape, or found I could not fix things myself. Then, I called on God.

I knew I was not leading a Christian life; moreover, I did not know what I should be doing. Christianity was labeled, in a box, all wrapped up and tidy.

I cried into the night, with Carole turning from one scripture to the next, allowing herself to be led by the Holy Spirit. The next morning, I quietly slid my door open to go to the kitchen and make coffee. Carole was already awake, sitting in the corner of the living room.

That morning, I asked Carole if she realized what had happened. We talked about how Carole thought she was coming on the trip for me, and I thought I was on the trip in order to help her. I told her how concerned I had been for her, and that when I received her email stating that she needed me, I was certain she had a big burden and needed a friend.

Carole declared that she did not send me such an email. I declare to you, I received one!

She also said she did not receive an email from me quoting the Apostle Paul. We like to believe that God played a joke on us, and set us up! He made the appointment and orchestrated the whole thing! We each thought we were meeting to help the other. But, God had something altogether different in mind!

The rest of our time together went pretty much as the first evening had, with Carole reading passages from the Bible to me, and me crying my eyes out. We went through forgiveness, love, mercy; and a host of other topics. I was like a sponge, Carole was my willing teacher, and the Holy Spirit was her guide.

We actually spent a couple of weeks together. It was a Bible Study Retreat, and He was there! I was almost afraid to come home; afraid I would never again experience His Presence. I did NOT want that experience to end!

Ever since that time, I have been continually aware of His presence. That beach trip affirmed my faith in God who is REAL, who LOVES me, who has PLANS for me, who CARES about things I care about, who is WITH me, and IN me, as close as the next beat of my heart!

Oh! Back to the emails. When I got home, I did not have my email to Carole in my emails, and there was no email from her saying she needed me. And, Carole did not have them either.

In the years since, He has taught me so much about living a Christian life. I am still learning; and there is no end in sight. My relationship with Him continues to go deeper and deeper, *"from glory to glory"*. (2 Corinthians 3:18).

Grace is everywhere!"

In Times of Trouble

Nahum 1:3 and 7 *"...the Lord hath his way in the whirlwind and in the storm, and the clouds are the dust of his feet. The Lord is good, a strong hold in the day of trouble; and he knoweth them that trust in him."* (KJV)

John 14:1 *"Let not your hearts be troubled. Trust in God; Trust also in me."* (NIV)

Hebrews 6:10 *"God is not unjust; He will not forget your work and the love you have shown Him as you have helped His people and continue to help them."* (NIV)

We often think about help, and who is going to help us. In times of trouble in our lives, we look about for someone to hold onto, someone to help us find a way.

We go to God for help spiritually, physically, mentally, and emotionally. We need help with our families, children, help at work, and help at church. We petition God continually for His intercession and assistance.

How often do we stop to think what God expects from us in terms of helping others? Are we secure enough to step out of our daily lives and offer help to others, even when we are in need ourselves?

A perfect example of this type of servitude comes from Cyndi Connery, whose spiritual journey led her through many desperate crisis situations, to a glorious awakening of her position as a Child of God.

Read Cyndi's story, and put yourself in her position for a moment.

"My mother was 20 years old and had four children. I was three years old when the State took us all away, we were split up.

From a very early age, I experienced the fear and loneliness of neglect and abandonment. On Sunday mornings, I would go with a neighbor and their kids to a local Church. I never knew what to do. No one told me or showed me how to pray; I did what everyone else did just because. I did not know why. I just wanted to belong somewhere.

I always felt different, not comfortable in my own skin. So, when I was introduced to drugs at the age of 12, for the first time I felt like I fit in. I continued using progressively harder drugs, isolating myself from my family, then eventually my friends.

The years slipped by – hard years of drug addiction. Finally, after 22 years of using on and off, I realized I had been trying to change the way I felt inside. Isolated, alone, scared. I finally reached bottom, with nowhere else to turn. There was not a drug powerful enough to overcome my despair. I was spiritually bankrupt. When I looked in the mirror, I had lost all sense of who I was.

I found help for my drug addiction through a Twelve Step Program that focused on Spiritual Principles as well as real help for the addiction. They talked about a Higher Power.

The 2nd step says, *"Come to believe that a Power greater than yourself can restore you to sanity"*.

I realized that, for all those years, I had a lower power, a dangerous force, driving me to continue using drugs. I had to find that Higher Power. I have always been one of those people who had to "see" things to believe them.

I struggled with the concept of faith in God as someone who would love and help me, considering all the wrong I had done, and more importantly, the way I felt about myself. Slowly, I started believing with hope, what people were telling me about God, and that He did not create me to toss me away like junk. I deserved to give myself a break.

The third step in the program is one where people can make a decision to turn their lives over to the care of God. I had struggled with this for so long, and wanted to feel that sweet inner peace of total acceptance and love that only a relationship with God can give

My husband and I took a trip to Lake Havasu, AZ, and there was a hot air balloon festival. We woke up one morning and saw all the beautifully colored balloons floating high above the landscape. It was surreal. We decided to chase those balloons, so we headed over to where they were going to be landing.

Watching them was such a freeing sight. I was alone, and I remember this one balloon with an Angel on it came down right in front of me. I felt as though I was in a time warp, and I know God was speaking to me in that moment in my heart. He said that he would come to me, be with me, when I needed Him in order for me to know and believe.

My faith in God and trust in Him began that moment, and has grown from that day. We took many pictures that day of all the balloons, not one of "my special angel balloon" showed up. It was no accident; that picture is forever burned in my soul.

Today, I have found my spiritual calling. I work to help women stop using drugs. These women use drugs as a way to cover their feelings. We work to raise their self-esteem, help them see the beautiful Child of God that they are. I let them know that I believe in them, and I share my experience so they know they are not alone and that they too can find peace, with themselves and with God.

I know I am right where I am supposed to be, doing what I am supposed to be doing. I have received many blessings. After 44 years, I was finally reunited with my siblings.

The ultimate was to be reunited with my God."

What an amazing story. God was with Cyndi, even when she did not feel His presence. He was always there. He preserved her for His service, and now she is helping others overcome the same desperate circumstances that she experienced.

Psalms 34:17 *"For the Lord is good, a stronghold in the day of trouble."* (KJV)

The Lord is a refuge for the oppressed, and will never forsake those who seek Him.

Overcoming the World

Revelations 3:21 *"To him who overcomes, I will give the right to sit with me on my throne, just as I overcame and sat down with my Father on His throne."* (NIV)

This is a tremendous promise verse. Just think about the true significance of this statement...Jesus said if we overcome, He will share His throne with us.

What a glorious moment it will be when Christ returns for those who believe in Him, establishes His kingdom, and reigns in power and glory. He invites us to join Him!

1 John 4:4 *"...greater is he that is in you, than he that is in the world."* (KJV)

Everyone who accepts Jesus has the power to overcome the world. The love of God strengthens us through the Holy Spirit, while Jesus intercedes for us in the throne room!

The Lord always provides an escape when we find ourselves in the midst of the battle. Overcoming is often a journey of the heart. As we trust and rely in Him, God strips away the layers. He is always faithful to answer our prayers, and lead us in the right direction.

Jesus wants us to overcome everything that could defeat us in our walk with Him. He is perfect example. And, through Him, nothing is impossible.

I Peter 5:8 *"Be sober, be vigilant; because your adversary the devil, as a roaring lion, walketh about, seeking whom he may devour."* But, Jesus gave us the power to overcome the enemy.

Luke 10:19 *"Behold, I give unto you power to tread on serpents and scorpions, and over all the power of the enemy: and nothing shall by any means hurt you."* (NIV)

Michele Beckner Atha and her husband, Bryon, have been missionaries to the country of Brazil for many years. I first met Michelle when she was a student at Piedmont Baptist College. Her humble and willing heart has allowed God to use her in reaching others for Him.

Michele talks of faith, honor, trust, and overcoming the world as she describes her favorite promise verse.

Job 23:10 *"But He knows the way that I take; When He has tested me, I shall come forth as gold."* (KJV)

"This verse has been a favorite of mine for years. When I was a high school senior at a Christian school in Virginia, Job 23:10 was chosen as our class theme verse.

At our graduation commencement, the valedictorian and salutatorian in their addresses that day divided the verse into two natural parts as a basis for the core of their message.

I was the salutatorian, and I spoke of how God will one day reward us for our faithfulness. Thus, we should always strive to remain faithful.

For many years though, the first part of the verse haunted me. As a missionary, especially when times were lonely or difficult, I assumed it was my "trial" or "test," and as such, I must accept it in all humility.

As I grow older, I find myself looking more toward the pearly gates, and reconsidering the thrust of this verse.

Yes, we suffer from time to time. No, this world will not get any better; but we have a hope and a future that makes our sojourn on earth worth it all. Christ gives us that hope and peace today, not just tomorrow.

He gives the hope that we need for each day to overcome the world's upheaval and environment. We can trust that God knows our predicaments and is always in control.

We can rest assured in knowing that this life is just temporary! We can make it through knowing that we shall see Him by and by."

Protection

Do you remember the little song, "*He's Got the Whole World in His Hands?*" As children, we learned the words, "*He's got you and me, brothers, in His hands. He's got you and me, sisters, in His hands. He's got the whole world in His hands.*"

Such a sweet little song used to illustrate God's continued presence in our lives. It is incredible that regardless of how old we are, we can still remember all the words to the song, as well as the tune!

We remember because the truth is in our hearts, and it has real meaning in our lives. God really does hold us in the palm of His hand. He provides for us, and protects us. He is always with us, and will never leave us.

He is the one we trust with our eternal soul. Life can sometimes be very difficult to bear, and we can feel overwhelmed with heartache. But, we can always depend on the everlasting and ever-sustaining love of God.

The Bible is full of promises that we can claim during those hard times that assure us of His eternal love and provision.

Psalm 25:20 "*Guard my life and rescue me; let me not be put to shame, for I take refuge in you.*" (KJV)

Proverbs 30:5 "*Every word of God is pure; He is a shield to those who put their trust in him.*" (KJV)

Psalms 91:10-11 "*There shall no evil befall thee, neither shall any plague come nigh thy dwelling. For he shall give his angels charge over thee, to keep thee in all thy ways.*" (KJV)

Jan Rogers is a precious lady in our church who loves the Lord, and sets an example of true faith in God. As she deals with a serious illness, she continues to praise God for His goodness to her and her family.

Here is Jan's promise verse, and her testimony.

Psalms 73:23,25-26 *"Nevertheless, I am always with You; You hold me by my right hand. Whom have I in heaven but You? My flesh and heart may fail, but God is the strength of my heart...forever."* (NIV)

"Having known the unconditional love of my daddy, I can accept the love of my Heavenly Father. I can even imagine climbing up in His lap when I feel small and vulnerable.

One of my fondest memories as a child is of walking hand-in-hand with Daddy. It didn't matter where we were going. I felt safe and secure, and just happy to be with him.

My Father-God has held my hand through some pretty tough times. There have been times that I have felt so alone, so unsure of the future, and I did not know what to do.

Through infertility and several miscarriages, He sustained me. That was the time I knew Him as the One who whispered in my ear and said that He would never leave me.

When it seemed my marriage would end, and I thought my heart was broken beyond repair, He showed me how to love again. He showed me how to be still and know, and He did mighty things that only God can do.

And now, as I am being treated for breast cancer, I have learned that I can trust Him with my very life. I know that He has always has my best interest in mind, and that He truly does *"work all things together for the good to those who love Him."*

I do not know how this latest challenge will end. But, I have learned that in those dark times when I am fearful, or do not know what direction to take, I can reach up and hold on to the hand of my Heavenly Father.

Although I cannot see where the next step will take me, I know that I can trust Him to take me safely where He wants me to go.

And I am happy, just to be with Him."

Purpose

Romans 12:2 *"And be not conformed to this world, but be transformed by the renewing of your mind, that ye may prove what is that good, and acceptable, and perfect will of God."* (KJV)

My sister, Sue, was almost two years old when I was born. She was an active child, blond, blue-eyed, and beautiful. *Active* is the operative word here. She was the first-born, and my Mother spent the first two years running after Sue.

Then along came me. I was an entirely different nature than Sue; not better or worse – just different. I was content to stay just about anywhere my Mother put me…in the crib, on a pallet on the floor, in the playpen. This made life much easier on my Mother because she was still running after Sue!

As I grew older, I spent a lot of time on the front porch. We had a covered porch with a glider-swing, and a little table. My Mother would put me on the porch and tell me to stay there. I would play for hours, making mud pies with real dirt and little tin pans and cups.

Every once in a while, my sister would go zooming by, running somewhere, running toward something, but usually running away from my Mother.

I remember very clearly how Sue would come whizzing around the side of the house at a full gallop. She would leap up on the porch, bounce off the glider, and jump to the ground off the back railing. She always hit the ground running.

I stayed on the porch, and rarely ventured out into the yard. The porch was safe; I was not an explorer, and was perfectly content and happy in my own little space.

There on the porch, I dreamed little girl dreams of what I wanted to do when I grew up. Most of all, I wanted to be a

Ladies of Grace

ballerina. But, I did not take ballet lessons, and the dream subsided into big girl realities of life

Suddenly, I was grown, married, with babies of my own. However, I was still sitting on the porch, figuratively speaking of course.

My life was so orderly and structured; I processed everything so carefully. I took care of the home, the children, taught Sunday School, sang in the choir, and did a hundred other things that Mothers do everyday. Yet, I was still dreaming dreams of things I wanted to do someday.

In my mind, and deep in my heart, I knew I was still on the porch. I was doing exactly what I thought was expected and required of me, and doing it well. But, I felt as if something was missing in my life.

It is interesting that my daughter, Marci, was experiencing the things that I had only imagined doing when I was a child. She started taking tap and ballet lessons when she was four years old. Every year there was a huge recital at Reynolds Auditorium.

Naturally, I was always there, sitting up front, with camera in hand. I was so proud as she came dancing out on the stage with all the other little girls, twirling and spinning with big smiles on their faces.

Marci had been taking dance lessons for two years, and it was time for the spring recital. The performance began, and the little girls came twirling on the stage. Marci was up there, spinning and tapping and bouncing away with all the other little six year olds.

Smack in the middle of all those little girls was a woman, probably 45 years old, wearing a tutu and leotard, and dancing her heart out. She danced, jumped, and tapped her way across that stage along with the children.

People were whispering, saying, *"look at that old woman up there. Who does she think she is; what is she doing up there?"*

But, as the recital progressed, this woman kept appearing, and it became obvious that she was thoroughly engrossed in dancing every step. By the end of the recital, people in the audience were cheering and applauding. I later learned that this woman's life dream had been to take dance lessons. She put aside her fear, and got up there! She danced her heart out.

As I watched this woman fulfill her dream, I realized that it is never too late to Dance! It is never too late to follow your heart, or follow God's gentle urging to do His will.

The point is....*Go Ahead and Dance*! Nobody cares if you cannot dance well. No one cares what you look like. Just Do It! Your friends will love you anyway. This woman fulfilled her deepest longing and at the same time, set a great example for those little girls.

I knew that it was time for me to jump down off the porch. Nobody was forcing me to stay on the porch, and I knew that God had a plan and a purpose for my life. I just needed to act on what He was telling me to do.

I began to overcome the inner resistance and fear, and the question, "*What if I fail*? So what if I do! It's OK. With God's help, I will try again.

And so, my story begins. I took a tiny step, then another. You can do it too. We all have inner strengths that build into our purpose. When we find out what we want to do, and we develop our talents to do it, and God blesses it, what a powerful combination.

I have talked to many women over the years who are waiting for "their turn". They tell me they always wanted to teach a class, paint a picture, travel, write a book, go back to school, and a host of other things.

I just ask them, "*What are you waiting for? If God is calling you to do it, then take a leap off the porch and do it.*"

Years from now, I want to look back on my life and know that I made a difference in someone else's journey. I want to follow every dream, and live every moment to the fullest. I want to go into Heaven sliding across Home Plate, not just showing up.

One of the most precious things I could ever hear in this life would be for my children say, "*You were a good Mom, and always there for me.*" And, to hear my husband say, "*I'm glad you are my wife.*"

When I leave this world, I want to hear from my Lord, "*Well done, my good and faithful servant.*"

I don't miss the front porch at all!

Strength

Isaiah 12:2 *"Behold, God is my salvation; I will trust and not be afraid: for the Lord Jehovah is my strength; He also is my salvation."* (NIV)

Isaiah 40:31 *"But they that wait upon the Lord shall renew their strength; they shall mount up with wings as eagles; they shall run, and not be weary; and they shall walk, and not faint."*

This is Regina Lane's verse. Her miraculous story is a testimony to God's sustaining strength throughout life's journey. This is Regina's story.

"All of my life, I have depended on God. Yes, there are times when I tried to depend on my own strength. But, looking back, the greatest decision I made in my life was to trust in the Lord Jesus at age five.

I believe in my heart that Christ will see me through any trial I encounter in my life, no matter what. It does not matter how old I am; I am confident that He is always with me!

There have been times when I did not understand why things happened, and all I could do was stand still, pray, and let God's will be done.

There was also a time when all I could do was pray because my life was in danger.

Jeremiah 33:3: *"Call unto me, and I will answer thee, and show you great and mighty things, which you do not know."* (KJV)

That is what I did. I called on my best friend. When I was 19 years old, my prayer and confidence in Christ gave me the strength to break free from a serial murderer and rapist. Twenty years later, I am able to tell my story of survival with Break Thru Films and HBO.

God poured his grace and mercy out on me. My only purpose in telling my story and sharing my faith is to give God the glory for the great thing He has done. I thank Him for allowing me to live a healthy and productive life.

I could be a bitter person for the way I was treated, and the horrible experience I suffered. But I am a better person by granting forgiveness to the people that hurt me."

Regina's extraordinary story is one of survival.

Isaiah 41:10 *"Fear thou not, for I am with thee; be not dismayed; for I am thy God. I will strengthen thee; yea, I will help thee; yea, I will uphold thee with the right hand of my righteousness."*

Ephesians 6:10-11 *"Be strong in the Lord and in the power of his might. Put on the whole armour of God that ye may be able to stand against the wiles of the devil."*

What kind of strength do you need? Endurance, patience, confidence, knowledge? Perhaps it's even physical strength, like Regina Lane

Whatever we need, the Lord our God is faithful to provide.

Trust

Proverbs 3:5-6 *""Trust in the Lord with all thine heart; and lean not unto thine own understanding. In all thy ways acknowledge him, and he shall direct thy paths."* (KJV)

There is no more qualified person to speak on trust than Linda Day Sears. She and her husband, Pastor Ed Sears, have faithfully served our church for over 28 years.

She is an excellent example of God's love as she cares for our congregation with grace and sincerity. She is a Bible Study Teacher, Ladies Ministry Advisor, and wise counselor and friend to all.

One of Linda's many attributes is her humor and quick wit. She has a gift of helping women maintain their grip on reality, and can quickly put life in perspective.

You will be blessed as your read her story.

"My life's verses are Proverbs 3:5-6. Throughout my Christian journey, I have relied on this selection of scripture many, many times.

"Trust in the Lord with all thine heart." It does not say to trust Him partially, or with some of our heart, but with <u>All</u> of our heart. Our trust has to be exclusive.

To trust in our own understanding is a natural tendency. Our flesh is weak. This is why we are warned to *"Lean not unto thine own understanding but in all thy ways acknowledge Him"* – one step at a time – in all ways great or small. We should take our concerns to Him.

We should go daily to our Father for guidance and direction *"for He shall direct our paths."*

We will never regret being led by the Spirit of God in our lives, even though we might not fully understand in this life.

The following story is about a time in my life when I trusted God to help me when I did not know which way to turn, or what to do.

Christian Cruising In Style

My husband and I love cruising, and have enjoyed several Christian cruises in the Caribbean. Our most recent trip was to Cozumel, Mexico.

Being very familiar with cruise embarkation and disembarkation procedures, we felt very comfortable on this trip.

On the last evening of our cruise, we were invited to a routine meeting for disembarkation. I decided to attend, even though I already knew what to do to prepare to get off the ship the next morning.

Just before retiring on that last evening of the cruise, we packed our luggage, and placed them outside our cabin door. Everything was in the luggage except what we would need to wear the next day. At midnight, the luggage was carried to the bottom of the ship.

After a good night of sleep, we awoke the next morning and began to dress before going to breakfast with our friends.

My husband was already dressed and waiting on me, since I am not a "morning person." I had packed a three-piece black jersey knit outfit – pants, top, and jacket, for the trip, and kept those out to wear off the ship.

I began to dress, and slowly pulled on my top. After looking around for my pants, I realized that I did not have them. My husband could see in my countenance that I was quite frantic.

He asked, *"What's wrong?"*

I said, *"I DON'T HAVE ANY PANTS!"*

Suddenly, he was in a state of shock. I was scared and began to feel a sickness in the pit of my stomach. I thought to myself, *"What am I going to do?"*

I could have wrapped the bed sheet around myself, but how dumb would that be? My husband offered to borrow a pair of pants from our neighboring cabin, but their luggage was also already in the bottom of the ship.

So, I began to cry out to God for help and guidance. God, the Holy Spirit, spoke to me in that still small voice.

He said, "*Linda, look at that jacket again.*"

I held it up and examined it closely. Remember, this jacket is made of very stretch jersey knit material.

I slowly placed my right leg in the right sleeve, and my left leg in the left sleeve. I buttoned up the front of the jacket, but still had the neck opening dangling between my legs.

Now, this was not a pretty sight, since I had this wad of material hanging down in the front! I quickly twisted the wad and tucked it into a "make-do" waist.

My husband gave me one of those *"I can't believe it"* looks, but it worked. Of course, he walked several steps ahead of me as we left the cabin to join our friends for breakfast.

Since I had to style and profile in this outfit for almost three hours, I tried to not be so obvious. But, many of the passengers on this ship were Pastors and their wives that we have known for a long time.

Needless to say, it was an extremely embarrassing situation. Finally, it was time to disembark the ship. This is a time when everybody is lined-up and ready to move in a big hurry.

As I was going down the gangway, my new attire began to slip downward. I was holding up the tail end of the jacket with one hand, and carrying my personal belongings with the other.

I yelled to my husband to locate our luggage and pitch my pants to me. He did just that, and I made my way to the ladies room to rectify my problem.

This was a horrifying experience at the time, but even in the little things, God is there.

Now we can laugh at what happened. I have shared and demonstrated this story at Women's Conferences and with many friends.

I will be sure to double-check my clothes on future cruises!"

Promises for Family

Beautiful

Proverbs 31:30 *"Charm is deceptive, and beauty is fleeting; but a woman who fears the Lord is to be praised."* (KJV)

After ten hours at work that day, standing in front of a classroom teaching Leadership Skills, I was mentally and physically exhausted. Yet, I spent another hour in the office reading emails, returning phone calls, and making lesson plans for the next day.

Climbing into my car, I happened to catch a glance of myself in the rear view mirror. *"Oh, no!"* My face looked just as tired as my body felt; my hair was askew, no lipstick, makeup worn off by the long day of work that began at 6 a.m.

Sighing, I hoped I would have time to freshen up a little before Dave got home from work. I started the car, and drove home, mentally ticking off the tasks I had to do that night, and wondering what I would cook for supper.

When I pulled into the garage and started to get out of the car, I heard Dave coming down the basement steps. He opened the door into the garage, and quickly walked over to the car to help me out.

In my mind I thought, *"Well, there he is, and I didn't have a chance to make myself presentable! Maybe it's dark enough in the garage that he won't notice how bad I look."*

As he pulled me into a big hug, I tried to bury my face in his chest so he would not see the circles under my eyes, and smudged eyeliner on my face.

Then Dave said, *"Babe, I know you must be tired, and I'm glad you are home. You are so beautiful to me. How do you do it after working all day?"*

Isn't God merciful? He made my husband just far-sighted enough that he could not tell that I really looked haggard! Dave was going on his mental image, not the reality standing in front of him.

Women judge themselves by the world's standard of beauty, which is unrealistic, and wrong.

A beautiful face, a graceful countenance, a perfect body – we want all those things. There is nothing wrong with that, and we should try to look our best, especially for our husbands.

Yet, we tend to put these things in the wrong perspective, and they become the source of our frustration. Many girls and women feel self-conscious, and lack self-confidence because they feel like they do not measure up to the world standard of beauty.

We miss the point entirely. God himself is the very essence of beauty, and He longs to share His beauty with us. Moreover, true beauty really has nothing to do with lipstick and hair.

When we accept Jesus as Savior, His beauty resides within us. The more we honor Him in our lives, the more we will mirror His beauty from the inside out.

1 Peter 3:4 *"...The unfading beauty of a gentle and quiet spirit, is of great worth in God's sight."* (NIV)

God says that constant focus on physical beauty is vain. Beauty is deceitful, and will fade away naturally, as we age. Instead, God tells us that true beauty comes from within.

Think about the women that God used as examples in the Bible. Consider Esther. Although Esther was very physically beautiful, she also had an inner beauty.

Esther won the King's favor and approval due to her beauty; and God's hand of protection was upon her as she yielded to His will. Esther understood the wisdom and power that comes from honoring God.

A woman that fears the Lord is beautiful. A church or body of believers that fears the Lord is beautiful.

God's eye is on us; His beauty is all around us. How much more beautiful could it get? His beauty is a place of honor and love.

Back to the garage. As Dave greeted me at the car that night, his loving comment was coming from a place of honoring me as his wife. The beauty he saw was not a result of looking at a work-weary face, but because he is a godly man, and he sees me through eyes of love.

That is the way God sees us – through loving eyes, and focused on our inner beauty.

The point is that God expects us to maintain our physical bodies the best we can; keep physically fit, and do those things to remain healthy and attractive. He does not want us slogging around, looking sloppy and unkempt.

Just remember that your true beauty lies within your heart, and will always outshine any outward beauty you possess.

And, thank God, our husbands sometimes forget to wear their "close-up" reading glasses!

Children

When I was a child, my Mother quoted scripture to me everyday. In her home, it was not unusual to have a Bible verse tossed out in answer to a question, to initiate discipline, break up a squabble, or even in response to a TV Commercial.

My Mother was so much into training her children in the ways of the Lord, that she monitored everything that came into the house, including commercials.

When I was growing up, alcoholic beverage and tobacco commercials were on TV, in magazines, billboards, and newspapers. The media promoted these products, and there was very little, if any regulation. Mom believed certain things were bad for her children, and so, to counter the influence of these commercials, she had a method.

Every time she saw an printed ad for an alcoholic beverage, she would rip the page out of the magazine or newspaper, throw it on the floor, jump up and down on it, while yelling, *"NO, NO, NO"*.

All four little sets of eyes would be focused on her – she had our attention! Then, she very calmly explained the dangers of becoming addicted to alcohol. Or, anything else she thought was wrong for us to do.

She prayed with us and for us. We were in Sunday School, Church, Wednesday night service, Vacation Bible School, Study Union, Sunbeams, Youth Clubs…and so on. Every time, everything, every service, we were there.

One Sunday night, my sister Sue decided she did not want to go to church. She wanted to stay home and watch television because "The Wizard of OZ" movie was playing.

She knew it would be useless to ask my Mother if we could stay home. Instead of asking, Sue concocted her own plan. She hid her shoes. She thought if she had no shoes to wear to church, she would not have to go.

We did not have several pairs of shoes like kids today own; we had one pair. My Mother looked everywhere for those shoes, but could not find them. What did she do? She marched Sue right out the door in her socks, straight up the aisle of the church, into the pew for Sunday night services.

My Mother, Mary Ruth Fox Day, is a kind and gracious lady, and I am so pleased that she agreed to share her thoughts on raising children.

"The Lord blessed me with four beautiful children; two girls and two boys. As all of you who have raised children know, there are joys and heartaches that come from parenting. Our desire is that these little ones will live perfect under our careful lists of do's and don'ts. We quickly forget that there is only one perfect and without sin, Jesus Christ.

I found that when I am through wringing my hands and saying, *"Where did I go wrong"*, I realize that we are all sinners and come short of the glory of God. Then the promise comes to mind, the one that I have claimed for all these years.

Proverbs 22:6: *"Train up a child in the way he should go, and when he is old, he shall not depart from it."* (KJV)

Mothers claim this promise, and as we see our children grow and come to the knowledge and acceptance of our Savior, we praise the Lord and know that He is good and that His love and mercy endures forever and to all generations!

And, finally, having come to many crossroads, not knowing which way to go, Proverbs 3:5 and 6 is the promise I claim. And, He has not failed me.

"Trust in the Lord with all thy heart and lean not unto thine own understanding. In all thy ways acknowledge Him and He shall direct thy paths." (KJV)

Parenting

There is an overwhelming sense of responsibility when you become a parent. My son, Todd, was born in a military hospital hundreds of miles away from my family. Hundreds of miles away from my mother!

I knew nothing about taking care of a baby. And, this baby was delicate; a premature baby weighing only a few pounds and with serious health issues.

He stayed in the hospital for weeks. My parents visited, but had to return home. So, when I was finally able to bring this baby home from the Intensive Care Nursery at the Hospital, I was so afraid I would do something wrong.

Truthfully, I did not even know how to put on a Pamper. I did not know anything about formula, sterilizing bottles, sleep patterns, what is normal and what is not. I learned everything the hard way with this baby. I was a wreck...on the phone with my mother continually. I did not know what to expect, what to do, what not to do. I learned "on the job".

I was in love with this child, overwhelmed by the responsibility, and I prayed continually! I knew my mother's favorite verse was Proverbs 22:6 and I took it seriously. But, I had questions. Primarily, what if I did it wrong?

How was I going to be responsible for this child's eternal soul through my training when I could not even figure out how to put on a Pamper! I had to get this right! How would I know what to do?

What did the Bible mean by the word *'train'*? What did the phrase *"when he is old"* mean? When he is 18? When he is 25? What is the right training? What happens if my child gets the wrong training? Does God honor the promise, even if I fail?

In my heart, I knew that there are no perfect parents and no one has the ideal home all the time. We are human, and therefore, we make mistakes. But, I wanted to do everything I could to make sure.

Circumstances in women's lives sometimes prevent them from being able to train their children as they wish. There are single parent homes, and divided homes. There are grandparents who are raising their grandchildren.

Unfortunately, there are parents who are simply unable to care for their children for a variety of reasons. Even when one parent is a Christian and trying their best to train the child, negative influences from others make it difficult.

Whatever the reason, there are homes that are not good environments in which to raise children. How are those children going to know God? Who is training those children?

God's word has the answer, and the promise. My Mother's verse, Proverbs 22:6 says, *"Train up a child in the way he should go, and when he is old, he shall not depart from it."*

That's it. It is our job to do the training. It is God's role to honor the promise. Therefore, I believe that, if a parent obeys God and sincerely tries to train the child, no matter what other influences are in that child's life, that child will not depart from what he or she was taught. God's word says so!

The New International Version of the Bible indicates "*train*" can even mean "*start*". Moses' mother only had enough time with her son to *start training* him in the way he should go. Yet God used him in a mighty way to rescue a whole nation.

Samuel's mother was the same. After pleading with God to give her a child, she willingly gave her young son back to God. He became a great man, greatly used of God.

If we do all we can to train our children to follow Him, God says they will not depart from it. We have His Promise! They can never get away from the wisdom we implant in their hearts and minds.

How does this work? God's part is to keep His promises to us, and He always does. Our part is to train – to be obedient to what He told us to do.

What if we make mistakes? We can still cling to the promises of God. Consider these promises:

Deuteronomy 6:5-7: *"Love the LORD your God with all your heart and with all your soul and with all your strength. These commandments that I give you today are to be upon your hearts. Impress them on your children. Talk about them when you sit at home and when you walk along the road, when you lie down and when you get up."* (NIV)

Isaiah 55:11: *"So is my word that goes out from my mouth: It will not return to me empty, but will accomplish what I desire and achieve."* (KJV)

1 Thessalonians 5:24: *"The one who calls you is faithful and He will do it."* (KJV)

As Mothers, our first responsibility is to love God. Then, we are to teach our children about God. We are to read it, talk it, love it, honor it, obey it, memorize it, and help them memorize it.

Everything from God's Word that we plant into their hearts and minds will stay there! Little by little as our children grow up, we train them. We have them for such a short time. They are grown in a snap. Make that time count.

If it were up to me to make sure that my children stayed with the program, then we would be in big trouble! Overwhelming failure!

However, GOD is the one who told us to train the children, and GOD is the one who promised us that, when they are old, they would not depart. God is faithful.

I am convinced that the farther they go, the more He will call to their minds the things they have been taught. He will NEVER let them go.

Just when that child begins to think about doing something wrong, WHAM! He will hear his Mother's voice telling him not to do it! I can still see my Mother jumping up and down on that magazine ad!

Ephesians 3:20-21 *"Now to Him who is able to do immeasurably more than all we ask or imagine, according to His power that is at work within us, to Him be glory in the church and in Christ Jesus throughout all generations, for ever and ever! Amen."* (KJV)

I love this verse! This is my Promise Verse for my children – the one I claim for them and my entire family.

Think about it – through <u>all generations</u>. My children, my grandchildren, their children, throughout the generations.

Lord, I cast all my kids upon you! The problem is that I keep taking them back! I am still trying to learn to give them up to God in prayer, and then stay out of it.

I cannot "save" my children. But, God can! He knows them…He knows where they are…He knows what they are doing…He has them in His hand.

There is another verse, Psalms 32:8 that states: *"I will instruct thee and teach thee in the way which thou shalt go: I will guide thee with mine eye."* (KJV)

He has His eye on my children – even now. Years ago, I would sit in the choir loft and my children would be seated on the fourth pew from the front where I could keep a good watch on them.

If they should happen to do something, start whispering, writing notes, giggling, or anything else that was inappropriate behavior for church service, all I had to do was give them "the look".

They knew exactly what "the look" meant. They knew that, if they did not stop whatever they were doing, I would come down out of the choir and sit with them. Once I caught their eye, I had their complete attention. The last thing they wanted was their mother stepping down out of the choir and embarrassing them!

Finally, remember that your child will eventually, God willing, grow up and leave you. Genesis 2:24: *"For this reason a man will leave his father and mother and be united to his wife, and they will become one flesh."* (NIV)

Start praying now while your children are young, that God will send the right person into your child's life. Pray for the person who is in charge of raising that special person who will one day be part of your family.

Our children are living in a world that seeks to destroy them with wickedness. They are faced with tremendous temptation and pressure everyday. They need our intercession with God through prayer.

And remember, the Prodigal Son **DID** return home!

Marriage

Claiming God's promises for marriage is critical, especially with the world espousing the lie that marriage is outdated, and the divorce rate, even for Christians, is over 50%. The fact that God established marriage "till death do us part" is passé in this environment of casual relationships and lack of commitment.

Your mate is for a lifetime. Your marriage deserves your utmost attention. Remember, one day your children will be gone. If you have not worked to develop and keep that intimate closeness with your husband, you will find yourself living with a stranger.

Verse 11 of Proverbs 31 says. *"The heart of her husband doth safely trust in her."* This means that our homes and families must be most important to us. When we think about God's will for our lives, we should make sure our husband has primary priority.

The husband of the virtuous woman in Proverbs 31 loves and trusts her unconditionally. It is more than being a good homemaker. A good wife is diligent in all areas; her home, her work, her children, and her spirituality.

She has a pure heart and a steadfast love. She works willingly, not because she "*has to*", but because she "*wants to*" please God and her husband. Her children call her blessed, and her husband praises her!

What woman would not love to hear her husband praise her? This husband told his wife that she was better than all others!

Proverbs 31:28, 29: *"Many daughters have done virtuously, but thou excellest them all."* (KJV)

Love is one of the most used and mis-used words in our language. It is packed with meaning, yet sometimes the word does not really seem to express what we want to say.

True and genuine love is a combination of the spiritual, mental, emotional, and physical response to another person. This kind of love will transform a ho-hum marriage into one full of delight and pleasure.

Couples need and want to feel a sense of belonging to each other. It is the kind of love that is essential in marriage; without it, there is no true place of security and safety in the union.

In marriage, couples should have a strong physical desire (love) for each other, and it is evident that the couple described in the Proverbs 31 scripture has that level of love. Although sex is not the most important aspect of marriage, it is a pretty good indicator of the health of your marriage.

The virtuous woman displays an unselfish, generous love that gives without expecting anything in return. She happily serves her husband, children, family, and others with love.

Claim His promises together; pray together. forgive each other. Live together harmoniously as an honor unto Him. Know that God is always there to help you, no matter what your circumstances.

Sisterhood

Titus 2:3-4 *"Likewise, teach the older women to be reverent in the way they live, not to be slanderers . . . but to teach what is good. Then they can train the younger women to love..."* (NIV)

There is something special about women helping women. My Grandmother, Lona Belle Pennington McKnight, is a precious example of that concept, and "sisterhood" was evident in her life as she served her family, neighborhood, and church.

We called her Maw Maw. She could do everything, and make anything from scratch. From biscuits to bedspreads, she had a talent for creating something from nothing. And, she made the most beautiful quilts you could imagine. Thankfully, she taught me how to quilt when I was a young girl.

Lovingly, my Grandmother would piece together her quilt top from scraps of fabrics left over from a variety of sewing projects. She was an excellent seamstress, and made her own clothes, dresses for her two daughters, and even shirts for her three sons.

After she completed each garment, she would gather the scraps of material and save them for a future quilt. Many times, she would cut and carefully piece together those scraps right away, making a "square" that would be used in a quilt top.

I remember brightly colored polka-dot swatches, checks, solids, stripes, and paisley, mostly of cotton fabrics, and all hand-pieced and hand-stitched together. When she had enough "squares", she would sew the quilt top together and get it ready for the 'quilting'.

Not many people know how to quilt the old-fashioned way. I am so thankful that she took the time and had the patience to teach me this craft when I was a little girl.

Several ladies from the neighborhood would gather at my Grandmother's house, including Mrs. Spann, Mrs. Holt, and sometimes Mrs. Martin. The large wooden quilting frame was setup in the dining room, and it filled up the entire space. Each woman would pull a chair up to the edge of the frame, and stretch the backing, batting, and lastly, the quilt top together and secure it tightly to the frame.

Then, the quilting began. Each woman, needle and thread in hand, would make perfectly sized stitches as she quilted the layers together. Chatter filled the room. These women could sew and talk at the same time. They did not even need to watch their needles; they knew "by touch" whether the stitches were right.

Maw Maw would stand behind me, and guide my hand as I learned to follow the chalk marks she made on the quilt top. She helped me make the stitches, and showed me how to keep the thread consistently tight enough to draw a good line.

Sometimes, she would inspect what I had sewn, and pull out the stitches if they were not done perfectly. Quilting stitches need to be the same length, using the same amount of tension on the thread, and with the same pressure pulling the layers together. If even one stitch is not right, it shows!

These women would work together on my Grandmother's quilt for several hours, and then depart to their own homes. It took more than one day to make and finish the quilt.

They had a special relationship – a sisterhood – that drew them close together. It was a close-knit neighborhood where people looked out for each other. Mothers were allowed to correct a child, even if it was not their child. Kids knew if they misbehaved, they were likely to be caught by one of the mothers. Neighbors cared about each other, and their well-being.

Afternoons might find them gathered on a neighbor's front porch to discuss the neighborhood needs, who was sick, who was having a baby, who had a death in the family. They took care of each other; they had a plan to help anyone with a need.

They had a regiment of providing meals to elderly people, taking care of each other's children, doing whatever was necessary to maintain a close community.

There were several local neighborhood churches, and most families attended one of them.

Ladies Circle Meetings and Sunday School Meetings were held in someone's living room. This closeness was essential to the growth of the local churches, and people respected each other's belief systems.

Deep friendships developed and lasted a lifetime. These women knew how to maintain their homes, love their husbands, raise their children, and grow the local church. Their devotion is an eternal testimony of sisterhood and benevolence to others.

What an awesome example of Titus 2. They taught others the importance of these things, and the value of a strong foundation in their church, families, and work. It was an excellent investment of their time.

I appreciate my Grandmother so much for allowing me to see this example. Humming some old gospel hymn, she would work from early morning to late evening, supported and loved by her wonderful husband, my grandfather, Ernest McKnight.

My generation has a much different method of communicating with each other. We no longer have time to visit on front porches, or talk over the backyard fence to find out that a neighbor is sick, or someone has a need. We use text messaging, email, and cell phones.

They invested significantly in each other, and we continue that heritage of investing in each other, just in a different way. They knew about serving, giving, and nurturing. They offered their examples to us by building strong families through the years, and strong church communities.

My Grandmother knew who she was in Christ. She passed that heritage to my Mother, and she passed it on to me. God willing, I will pass it to my children and grandchildren.

Develop a compassionate servant heart, like the example of the virtuous woman in Proverbs. She, just like my Grandmother, shared her wisdom and achievement with others.

The Greatest Promise of All

Salvation

John 3:16-17 *"For God so loved the world, that He gave His only begotten son; that whosoever believeth in Him shall not perish, but have everlasting life. For God sent not His son into the world to condemn the world, but that the world through Him might be saved."* (KJV)

Most people learn these verses at a very young age. But, do they really grasp the power of the message? This is God's promise to us that there is salvation through Jesus Christ.

It talks of God's mercy, and promises us eternal life. What better reward could there possibly be than to live with the Father forever!

When you quote the verse, put the emphasis on the word 'so.' God **SO** loved the world…He loved us, continues to love us, **SO MUCH** that He sacrificed His only son.

What an awesome, amazing thing to do! Can you imagine giving your only son for the life of someone else?

Then, put emphasis on the word 'whosoever.' This is a free gift to anyone who believes. It is the Greatest Promise of All.

1 John 1:9 *"If we confess our sins, He is faithful and just to forgive us our sins ,and to cleanse us from all unrighteousness."* (KJV)

Acts 16:31 *"Believe on the Lord Jesus Christ, and thou shalt be saved and thy house."* (KJV)

There are no age restrictions, no other requirements or works or sacrifices. Even young children can understand the word of God, and accept Jesus into their hearts.

Becoming a Christian does not require any grand spectacle. You do not have to run down a church aisle, scream and cry, or make a great speech or proclamation.

Salvation is a matter of the heart. God said that if you believe in your heart, confess your sins, and accept Him, you will be saved.

Romans 10:9 *"If you confess with your mouth the Lord Jesus, and believe in your heart that God raised Him from the dead, you will be saved."* (KJV)

Biblical conversion is as simple as that. Romans 8:16-17 *"The Spirit itself beareth witness with our spirit, that we are the children of God. And if children, then heirs; heirs of God, and joint-heirs with Christ; if so be that we suffer with him, that we may be also glorified together."* (KJV)

Galatians 3:26 *"For ye are all the children of God by faith in Christ Jesus."* (KJV)

Indeed, we become God's Children. We are immediately adopted in God's family when we accept Christ. We have a new relationship, and we are given all the responsibilities and privileges of a Child of God.

One of these privileges is being lead by the Holy Spirit. The Holy Spirit is our witness, and His presence in our lives encourages us with God's love.

Romans 5:5 *"God poured out His love into our hearts by the Holy Spirit, whom He has given us."* (KJV)

Our Heavenly Father's love is always with us, and nothing can separate us from Him.

John 10:27-29 *"My sheep hear my voice, and I know them and they follow me. I gave unto them eternal life, and they shall never perish; no one shall ever snatch them out of my hand. My Father, who has given them to me, is greater than all; no one can ever snatch them out of my Father's hand."* (NIV)

This is the most precious promise!

Read what Mary Day has to say about salvation.

"The Lord has blessed me so, how can I possibly praise him enough? I accepted Him as my Savior as a child of ten, not fully understanding all, but knowing that I had given my heart to Jesus. I knew that I belonged to Him.

Now, as an 80 year-old woman, I have lived a long life, and have trusted Him all the way, even when in doubt. I have claimed His promise in Romans 19:9, *"If that shalt confess with thy heart the Lord Jesus, and shalt believe in thine heart that God hath raised Him from the dead, thou shalt be saved."* (KJV)

And, in verse 13, *"For whosoever shall call upon the name of the Lord shall be saved."* (KJV)

Mary's story is precious, and just one example of God's mercy and salvation in a young person's life. I was saved at the age of five, in the living room of our home, being led to Him by my mother, Mary Day.

Years later, I had the joy of leading my own children to Him, and my grandchild. God extends His salvation to everyone who believes in Him.

Romans 1:16 *"I am not ashamed of the gospel of Christ; for it is the power of God unto salvation for everyone who believes."* (KJV)

Heaven

2 Corinthians 5:6-8 *"Therefore, we are always confident, knowing that, whilst we are at home in the body, we are absent from the Lord. For we walk by faith, not sight. We are confident and willing rather to be absent from the body, and to be present with the Lord."* (KJV)

A glimpse of Heaven! We know that when we die, we will instantly be with God. To be "absent from the body – present with the Lord." How glorious that will be! Further, we know that we will see our loved ones again.

1 Thessalonians 4:15-16 *"For this we say unto you by the word of the Lord, that we which are alive and remain unto the coming of the Lord shall not prevent them which are asleep.*

For the Lord himself shall descend from heaven with a shout, with the voice of the archangel, and with the trump of God: and the dead in Christ shall rise first. Then we which are alive and remain shall be caught up together with them in the clouds, to meet the Lord in the air: and so shall we ever be with the Lord. Wherefore, comfort one another with these words." (KJV)

We do not need to be full of sorrow as others are, those who do not know the Lord. Just imagine how extremely painful it must be to experience the death of someone you love, and not be certain that they are saved.

The souls of departed Christians are already with the Lord, and He will bring them back when He returns. Their bodies will be reunited with their souls, and those of us who are still alive on this earth will be called up together with them. And, we will forever be with the Lord.

There is no more comforting knowledge than this. We are saved; eternally bound to God forever. When we die, we are immediately escorted to Heaven. We will be reunited with our loved ones.

My father, Joe Fox, Sr., and I used to sing a song together, "*What a Day That Will Be.*" The chorus of the song says, "*When I look upon His face, the one who saved me by His grace. What a day, glorious day, that will be.*"

Who are you longing to see again? What a grand reunion day that will be!

How to Find God's Promises

Hebrews 10:23 *"Let us hold unswervingly to the hope we profess, for He who promised is faithful."* (KJV)

Everyone knows about promises; from seeing promises made, and unfortunately, seeing them broken. Most everyone has, at some point in their life, broken a promise to someone else

There are many reasons why this happens. Sometimes we forget; sometimes circumstances are beyond our control. People change their mind, and break their promises.

A broken promise can be devastating! Someone promised to be faithful to you – but was not. Someone promised to pay you back – but did not. What we learn from an early age is that a promise is not worth anything if you cannot trust the person who is making the promise.

We can rest assured that the promises of God are real. Every promise of God is true.

There are thousands of promises in the Bible. Some of these promises were made specifically to a person for their own purpose. An example of this would be when God promised a son to Abraham and Sarah.

Other promises are there for everyone who believes in Him. Such as the promise to never leave or forsake us in Hebrews 13:5b. And, the promise to return for us in John 14:3.

He promises to supply every need we have. Philippians 4:10 *"But my God shall supply all your needs through Christ Jesus."* (NIV)

That does not mean He will give us everything we want, all the luxuries of life. It means He will give us what we need. Like the story of Jackson in a previous chapter. Jackson did not **need** to be Spiderman – he **needed** to be Jackson!

He promises that His grace is sufficient for us in 2 Corinthians 12:9. He promises that we will not be overtaken with temptation, and that He will provide a way to escape.

1 Corinthians 10:13 *"There hath no temptation taken you but such as is common to man: but God is faithful, who will not suffer you to be tempted above that ye are able; but will, with the temptation, also make a way to escape, that ye may be able to bear it."* (KJV)

God promises us so many things, including eternal life. We can rely on His promises when we need comfort and assurance.

How do you find a promise? Listed here are a few steps that will help you search the Bible to find the promise you need in your life.

1. Look in the concordance of your Bible for a key word, such as strength, courage, comfort.
2. Read the scripture references for that word or phrase. You will see other words and phrases that are similar and connected. Research those as well.
3. Use online research resources to scour the Bible for promises. Try www.crosswalk.com and use their Bible study tools.
4. Ask God to show you the promise He has for you in your situation.

God delights in taking care of His children. If you are a child of God, and living in His will, He will fulfill His promises to you.

Psalms 145:13 *"The Lord is faithful to all His promises and loving toward all He has made."* (NIV)

About The Author

Dr. Linda F. Felker

Dr. Linda F. Felker is the President of Felker Consulting, Inc. She provides professional development analysis, corporate leadership training, consultation, authoring, and counseling. She holds a charter certification to administer the Myers Briggs Type Indicator and conducts couples, individual, and group counseling sessions on psychological and personality type in relationships.

Linda is a frequent guest speaker at leadership and women's conferences across the country and is the author of several books, including *Lessons From the Purple Tree, Homewreckers,* and *Giggles in the Garden.*

She and her husband, David, have three children, Todd, Marci, and Brent, and two grandchildren, Zachary and Jackson. She is a charter member of Grace Baptist Temple.

Printed in the United States
143281LV00002B/1/P